# CRASH & BURN

# *Crash* & *Burn*

## Michael O'Neill

PUBLICATIONS
2019

Published by Arc Publications
Nanholme Mill, Shaw Wood Road,
Todmorden OL14 6DA, UK
www.arcpublications.co.uk

978 1911469 66 7 (pbk)
978 1911469 67 4 (hbk)
978 1911469 68 1 (ebk)

Cover image:
EUGÈNE DELACROIX, Tasso in the Madhouse
(Tasso in the Ospedale di Sant'Anna in Ferrara) 1839.
Oil on canvas. In the Oskar Reinhart Collection,
'Am Römerholz', Winterthur

ACKNOWLEDGEMENTS
Acknowledgements are due to the following publications
and their editors in which poems have already appeared:
*British Prose Poetry*, ed. Jane Monson (Palgrave, 2018), *London
Magazine, The Reader, Refractions: Romanticism, Modernism,
Comparitism: Essays in Honour of Peter Vassallo*, Ivan Callus,
James Corby and Maria Frendo, Msida [Malta]: Midsea, 2019).
'Maltese Wafers' quotes phrases from volume 2 of *The
Notebooks of Samuel Taylor Coleridge*, ed. Kathleen Coburn
(Princeton University Press, 1961). 'You and One' quotes
phrases from John Haffenden, *William Empson: Volume 2:
Against the Christians* (Oxford University Press, 2006). The
third section of 'Candles' quotes a line from Percy Bysshe
Shelley, 'Hymn to Intellectual Beauty'.

Editor for the UK and Ireland:
John Wedgwood Clarke

*For Posy, Daniel, Melanie
and Millie*

This volume covers medical treatment of an illness – cancer of the oesophagus – diagnosed in September 2017. Following diagnosis and staging (the theme of the final poems in *Return of the Gift*, Arc, 2018), the treatment fell into three main phases (corresponding to this volume's sometimes overlapping three sections): a course of neoadjuvant chemotherapy (involving emergency hospitalisation during the first of three cycles); the decision to operate, the operation, and the immediate aftermath; convalescence after leaving hospital and a further course of adjuvant chemotherapy (stopped after two cycles).

I would like to thank many doctors and nurses at the University Hospital Durham, the Royal Victoria Infirmary in Newcastle, and the Freeman Hospital in Newcastle, and at the Claypath Medical Practice in Durham, for their professional expertise and care.

A poem in the volume's Coda alludes to the fact that fears expressed in 'Scoping' and 'Recurrence' were subsequently realised.

I owe a special debt of thanks to Tony Ward and Angela Jarman at Arc, most enabling of editors.

*Michael O'Neill*

# CONTENTS

## I

## II

CODA

I

## FALSE POSITIVE

'Good news' – she says on the phone, this sensibly
    downbeat nurse,
who's schooled me in the school of knocks that are hard,
so that I'm still braced, even after I've heard
to the contrary, to learn that the feared metastasis

has been confirmed by the MRI scan,
the worst of the lot, as, layer by sliced layer,
my dodgy left hip was investigated from position
after position for more than an hour

until, bladder filling, I planned to haul
myself out of that cacophonous contraption
head first, and make a run for it, escaping all
further help and intervention from then on,

taking refuge in a bar with a bottle of whisky, a crate of wine...
'Good news; what we hope will be curative chemo can begin.'
I've been warned already that, even should this joyous event
    happen,
I'll be scanned later on for signs of disease progression.

## SOLILOQUY

*(for Robert Carver)*


Day 17, cycle 1,
neoadjuvant chemo:
I've begun to weaken,

although I still go
to work, teach, try to carry
on without bravado.

Today, trying to lug my
handouts down the street
almost dropping my burden, I'm helped by

this knight-like friend, met
by chance along my via dolorosa...
He cleaves a passage through throngs that wait

for thoughts about the hero's aporia
(to be or not to be – nice to have a choice);
ensures I'm able to set about the lecture.

I cope, draining insipid juice,
just about, tempted to misquote
last words as 'The rest is sickness'...

The moment it's over, I speed off to vomit
in the gents, wave upon wave
rising from my gut.

It's going badly; something has to give.

## CRASH AND BURN

'Febrile neutropenic sepsis'
said the doctor who seemed six feet six
as he stood at the end of the bed
and greeted me at 6 am – so many sixes –
following the recognition the night before
that I couldn't go on: 'you've 0.4 white cells
and no immune system' the observant,
steady-nerved oncology nurse will tell me.

'Crash and burn': muttering through warped lips, I was
Icarus spiralling like a downed fighter plane.
I thought I was still compos mentis
but the dreams were primordial, flamed round my skull.
After three or four days of barely drinking
for myself (any fluid was being dripped),
I managed a sip of tea
in the small hours and thought I'd just drunk nectar.

The strong hospital brew entered my gullet
like a potion concocted by the gods.
I stopped at the threshold beyond which I must not venture,
facing the nurses who talked off and on
at their central desk, opposite my room.
I stood at the doorway and whispered hoarsely,
'I feel like Oliver Twist but could I have more please'
– which got me a laugh and another cuppa.

Mission completed, I climbed back into bed.
'Sleep now', ordered the kind Filipino nurse;
'you've not slept for three nights. You must sleep.'
I was happy to obey, finally able to unfurl my limbs,
the ache dying that had run from throat to stomach
in a system of pain they'd just about worked out

with several medicines how to defeat.
I lay there; instead of pain there came light,

a blinding Catherine-wheel of light, and then
a dizzying, relentless army of images
that seared their life on my pyretic brain.
Every page I'd ever read of Dickens,
all his rhythms, solemn when needed as at the end
of *Little Dorrit*, but feverish, too, gathering
hints and details into one cumulative push
– every page I'd ever read by him galloped

past me in a printer's devilish riot,
insisting I read it with sensitive care,
even as each page whirled on to the next page,
a Manichean blizzard of paper, fonts and type
that overwhelmed my struggle to attend
as I knew I must until I woke in fear of the words
that rolled like heads beneath my bed, and a body
came in, switched on the light, injected me.

## SOCKS

He was not, he told me, a nurse,
tried to shake my hand.
I declined – 'neutropenic'.
Not sure he could understand,

but he didn't seem put off his stride
as he advised about cutting socks
at the top where they restrict
blood-flow and cause oedemic blocks.

He asked whether I'd been under
pressure over the last year.
I gave him the kind of heartfelt
outpouring you find in drama

that brings out how little we
listen to one another. Stirred
by my tale of self, I heard him
counsel, 'Dodge stress; be cured',

before asking whether I'd mind if
he cut my socks at the top
which is one key area I'd gone wrong,
he felt, urging me to stop

in their tracks life-damaging things
I'd been doing to myself for a decade
or more and change my priorities.
It made me smile. 'Cut away', I said.

## VIEW

It had a view, the room I was condemned
and lucky to inhabit for two weeks.
I'd move closer, as my white cell count climbed,
to the window, read my Milton – no idea why
I brought him (certainly bemused the nurses) –
and stare with a tired longing at the sky.

Vallombrosa, its fallen leaves a truth
too much for me, recalled our honeymoon visit,
the fictive sadnesses of distant youth
no longer bearable as I turned
to watch a car circle a roundabout and come back
down the road it had seemed to leave behind.

And yet, though sometimes uninspired, the view
was still a view, spoke of a realm elsewhere
in which light and sky might conjure a new
series of manifestations, healing spaces,
a glimpse of chance escape from illness, even
a made-up Eden thronged by angels' faces.

## SPILL

You leant back, Botticellian
as always, in a chair
in my isolation room,
wearing the mandatory
apron and gloves with
considerable style, then
jumped to your feet and
started moving about
restlessly. I wanted
to say, 'Just be still; it's
a cure to look at you',
but communication
was difficult: I'd
virtually lost my
voice, thanks to the thrush
creaming my throat.
In the end, we wrote
notes to one another,
poignant as missives stored
in an old mahogany desk
with pigeon-holes and side-panels,
forgotten love-letters...
You were so anxious
about me, my heart hurt –
that's no figure of speech –
even when, trying to help,
you knocked over
a jug of water on
my bedside table,
before you had to go,
my sheets and clothes soaked through
as the next nurse in
noticed straightaway: 'Only
my wife', I said, 'emptying

the jug over me.' 'You
probably deserved it',
she laughed as she got me
sorted; left alone,
I murmured *I'll never
deserve you,
never.*

**TEST**

Being ill
makes you feel

how holy
the body

and soul are
their desire

conjointly
sacredly...

Being well
is to call

an end to
the old view

a grim test
is the best

## CARNIVAL

Chords crashing and meshing in 1972,
New York; celebration wailing like lament:
'... she's walking through the clouds'
– a figure sent to, meant to, haunt.

She's still somewhere close
you find, listening to Clapton and co
for the first time in a very long time,
a face returning as you start to go

towards the shades and stage a carnival
of sorts, bidding farewell to lips and eyes,
lissome hallucinations of desire,
how the moon rose, that night, behind drugged trees.

## VISITORS

Out of hospital and indeed in it
while I experienced each draining night,
I've been given the gift of visit after visit
by friends who manage awkwardness just right,
even tolerating, one or two, my grim
bouts of nausea when I was first admitted.
I'm often tired, but revive at seeing them.
In fact, I discover I'm ideally suited,
which surprises me, to the attentions of those
ready to share a joke, an observation, a small glass,
who let me go on about my plans,
as though our existential dimensions
were the same, as though we occupied
the same place in which none of us has died.

## TORTURE

Sleep was impossible when
that man would begin
to imitate (one hoped) the groans of the dying,
his personal Passchendaele.

A low growling would heighten,
climbing a tormented scale
towards a top note of pain, then turn
to a sob as anguish heaped again.

Please give him something, anything,
I'd mouth, enduring another night.
He seemed beyond care; attempts were made,

judging from the fret
outside my isolation room, but nothing
could stop him torturing the ward.

## FOOT DROP

Thanks chemo for another gift:
inability to flex my left foot
in an upward direction.
For a few days I lurch, bereft
of guidance, an orphaned, new-born,
jumble-limbed beast; veer from the straight.

The damage runs back and up
to the peroneal nerve
in the calf, behind the knee.
Cisplatin may have to take the rap;
seems the cure is to wait; be brave;
strap an orthotic device on and see

what happens as the weeks pass.
I fear I'll be half-lame for ever,
but invest in an elegant cane,
strut around like a dandy whose toes
are riddled with gout, and offer
half-prayers sensation will return.

## NEW YEAR'S DAY

Chemo starts to figure
as a double-tongued serpent's kiss,
as a treacherous seducer
who may keep you alive.

This New Year's Day
I've hardly eaten,
taken to my bed at noon
with nausea and fatigue

and haemorrhoids so painful
it's as though a dagger
has been thrust into my anus
for the pure hell of it.

Two more days
to endure, then day 1
– my new Robespierrean calendar –
of cycle 3. Treat in store!

Off to the GP tomorrow
in the hope these latest
side effects can be 'managed'.
Chemo, my dark fate.

## POISON AND CURE

On a reduced dose now
I've got to the midpoint
of chemo cycle 3.

'Poison and cure;
cure and poison;
poison and cure.'

My mantra as
I down six tablets
twice a day.

It'll be more
than OK to leave
this time behind

before I sullenly
yield my tumorous
foodpipe to the

savage, healing blade.

## NEW JEANS

ECX saps the appetite. I've lost weight,
so much so I patronised a shop
I'd never normally go near and bought
a costly pair of jeans. Just couldn't stop

myself from what I've not often done
before (eye up clothes) – and left
as well with a belt that helped my lean,
new figure limp on upright. Sad, to gift

racked limbs with smart attire exactly when small
signs of joy flickered, yet blindly resilient,
too, I think, my own monitor, the drive to cope with change.

'I placed my faith in Hugo Boss', I smile
when a friend notes my brushed, blue kecks; 'spent
wastefully in the effort to feel less strange.'

## MALTESE WAFERS

*(for Peter Vassallo)*

'Hard to express that sense of the analogy or likeness of
a thing which enables a symbol to represent it so that we
think of the thing itself, yet knowing that the thing is not
present to us',
    COLERIDGE, *Anima Poetae.*


1

WITH HIM

Guts in agony, the latest side effect
(undignified, all too real),
I trawl through his notebooks,

that suffering wanderer
with his colic, painful bowels
and memories of a vanishing face,

and I'm with him there in the brilliant gardens,
taking in the evening gun salute, its 'Rings of Russet'.
With him I endure the Baptist's dark beheading,

delight in the blinding limestone magnificence
of the forts, churches and palaces,
the 'dazzling Cotton Sails' on the Med's *'perfect* Blue',

the 'pretty Jewesses' and the moon
'dim-glimmering thro' the dewy window-pane',
and find some sleep from somewhere, dream of ships

entering or exiting the Grand Harbour, drawing
my secondhand, second sight through long wakes,
the present moment briefly all that matters.

2

SIMULACRUM

The fine view
above St Julian –

'the grand curving Harbour';
'the one Tongue of Land':

how well he knows
his new topography;

how well he embodies
the spark that jumps

between pain
and sharp observing...

Malta, sacred space for me,
allowing a simulacrum of his

plural-minded search,
ostrich eggs crushed underfoot,

some hatching noiselessly, sensation
finding utterance, 'outering' in words.

3

SOLACE

In the midst of illnesses
isolation half-bigoted recoil
from idolatrous images
the governor's wife

noting in that cold-hearted way
in which stereotypes continue
to stereotype themselves his odd 'impatience'
about whether letters from loved ones had arrived

in the midst of such things the sight
of the moon or sun or sea
their particular appearances
the solace they offer still holds

4

Like Aeneas surrounded by Carthage's
noble, half-topped towers, he tells his wife,
constructing a rope-bridge between the ages.

Then as now, building work might leave
that impression, though after darkness starts to pour,
Valletta's monumental defences have

a different effect. As he saw.
A 'monstrous fortification' – yes,
if you grant 'monstrous' a core

or peripheral meaning of 'marvellous'.
A place to draw your thoughts together,
a shadow-ridden, De Chirico place.

'Dreary' he calls the island, yet the weather,
the blue heat, agrees with him, as does
the way 'you almost see things grow', 'the caper

(most beautiful of flowers)' profuse
in 'the high walls and battlements',
their tall 'interstices'.

His time, my time – neither complements
or cancels the other; hard to ensure his voice
even as it yearns for response

30

doesn't turn into fodder for personal choice,
a mask for what I wish to evoke,
but if Valletta recalls Dido's Carthage, let his

relish for experience improve unfinished luck.

5

*WHOLENESS*

'now the Maltese Wafers for instance /
that stick to your mouth and fingers
almost so as to make it impossible
to get them off without squeezing them
into a little pellet, and yet will not stick to the paper'

This is meant to 'evidence the superiority of English artisans'
but I'm not convinced that's the effect of the entry,
which speaks, to my ears, of how the new place has begun
to live in the poet's attuned sensorium, to stick
to his mouth and fingers, to inhabit his thoughts

that take their bearings from his decision one evening
to place 'three pieces of Wood' on a 'nice bed
of glowing Embers', to stay up late and grapple
with 'restlessness', its *fragmentary* nature' and 'connection'
to '*Wholeness*', that elusive grail.

## PORT MEADOW

That wintry light ensouling Port Meadow –
common ground that has never been ploughed
for at least 4000 years –
propelled itself through a prism of shadow.

The wide sky, the flood plain, the geese,
the emptiness that seemed to swallow brisk walkers
and fluorescent runners,
the cold that made my gloveless fingers freeze

as we discussed my forthcoming trials
(under the knife in a month or so when I'm likely to be
opened, resected, and stitched up),
exhaustion after the recommended miles.

We crossed the river, then the extended bridge
that spans the added railway line, after which
the walk I've taken many times,
and then we reached the edge

of the Meadow, headed back to
habitation, a fire, warmth,
conversation, laughter, memories,
the hope one might pull through.

## APPETITE

The bowls of soup
as though I were running a soup-kitchen for one;
the pots of yoghurt, dug into with a long spoon
as, unavailingly, I tried to fill myself up –

that's essentially all I had eaten
since the chemo regimen began
what seems a dynasty ago,
dealing appetite a poisonous blow,

until a brace of Sundays back
when a lamb dinner vanished, the rack
of meat cleaving itself from the bone,

and, for an hour, I rejoined a world
where people swallow freely, and complain
their wine's been insufficiently chilled.

## CHARM

The lines I removed
as over-explicit
the other day
rise up in my throat:

*… and want to be*
*conscious, to exist*
*whatever the price,*
*not to have missed*

*whatever the future*
*might realise itself as,*
*a star that shines like cold fire,*
*or an uninhabited house.*

So I resurrect them here
to serve as a charm
that might ward off fear,
accommodate harm.

## SCOPING

The mainstays grow unstable,
the rope-bridge unreliable.

A few weeks in port, taking stock,
then you're hoisting the torn sail again...

Job's latest comforter:
'If it comes back you're done for'.

The merest niggle seems a paper
marked with an ill-omen.

It'll pass but you don't forget it,
the swaying, the pitching, the heart's worst fright,

the anxious scoping of the shore
to see if that path you were able to walk

is still visible, to check whether
your plan's a dud or might still work.

# II

## POST-CHEMO CT SCAN

Another scan. And yet the first in
months and possibly the one that counts the most.
As per instruction, I've not eaten
for hours, not even a mouthful of toast.

Just sitting in the waiting room, just praying
nothing untoward shows up
to scupper plans to operate, the operating
table my worst fear and likeliest hope.

I took the train earlier. The sky,
a cold February sky, with no concern
for those who search for answers to the why
and wherefore, began to burn

with a blue intensity, an iced flame.
That's all outside now, in the world from which
cancer keeps me, trapped in a waiting room,
waiting for dye and contrast, image-rich

evidence, waiting for a scan,
computerised tomography that will unveil
secrets of thorax, chest and abdomen,
my tumour-ridden, too material soul.

## HURDLE

### 1

'The course of cancer never did run smooth'
you say, with an attempted smile.

Will they operate?
Will I be given only palliative chemo,
poisoned until the deferred event occurs?
Will I kick the inevitable bucket?

Late February sunlight is warmer
and softer, and allows me seatage at
a table in this garden, recovering
from the severities of winter.

### 2

Which might return,
offset the hard-won hopes
of this in-between season.

A 'varied' CT scan report,
food starting to stick once more
but, as luck veers again,
and only after I've swung
from a gallows in limbo
when a phone-call raised
a two-day fear that the op
would be off because
disease may have progressed
(the large node turned
out to be harmless),
the team finally decides

to excise the tumour, resect
my errant foodpipe,
remove the hazardous lymph nodes

– after, of course, the pre-op assessment, less,
this one, of a hurdle to crash your shins against,
still a hurdle, though, especially the ECG,
but one I leave unknocked behind.

## TRUCE

Just a few days
before the op

I've taken us
all to Grasmere

in late February
ancient presences

the fells bask
magnified in the

clear blue
sunlight

that falls on stone
and thought

like a brief
hint of a truce

Helm Crag
Stone Arthur

Silver Howe
Seat Sandal

benign aloof
watchful

leaning forward
as though to

give me a
gauche group hug

## CHILL

In it howled, the Beast from the East,
a monster bringing snowy drifts
and a bloodless chill. I had turned and tossed
most of the night, awaiting surgical crafts
and arts, getting up at five. Bag by the door,
I looked out for the taxi's coming.
It arrived, heroically. Numbed to the core,
I said goodbye, caught a bird's solitary song,
then headed towards gown, consent form, and
anaesthetic at the base of the spine
after we'd laboured down a motorway whitened
to the essence of white, the headlamps' shine
a weak halo superimposed upon a new
and featureless, near-impassable view.

## HDU

The night lights burn on in the High Dependency Unit.
A living man can resemble a corpse,
I think, looking at each bloodless digit,
conscious of tubes and drains.

*

I keep imagining –
the opiates, I suppose – I'm on the set
of some spun-out, relentless melodrama, some
equivalent to 24. It's not a ward, but
a prison; I'm not a patient, but shackled
to a bed against my will, having committed
I know not what transgression… One morning
the young nurses are teenagers getting ready
for the day, eating breakfast in a communal house
into which the set has been transformed.

*

Without my temporarily confiscated phone,
there's no knowing whether it's day or night
in this windowless place I begin
to accept must be real, with its ward rounds,
smiling, joshing faces, telling me I'm doing well.
Yet, back from another op, I ask, 'Where am I?',
a question shrugged off as absurd…
I dream I'm driving across the M62,
desolate moors veering away into the darkness.

*

Gradually the drugs wear off. I learn
where I am, my anchor a mark on the wall
that stays the same. There are others in this place.
They ring their buzzers, cry out in their sleep or moan.
Nurses – not phantasms – come to our aid.

## REFUGEE

One sees him propped up there, exhibiting
the tough bravado of a frightened child
that masquerades as courage of a sort.

He shifts, turns. He writes still but cannot sing.
The morphine keeps him acquiescent, mild,
tawdry mortality his constant thought.

It's observation time again. BP
and temperature are measured, jotted down.
He acts as though the tests were not for him.

He stirs each morning like a refugee
from his own life, a stranger in a gown,
surgically altered, nails needing a trim.

Mann, modern Goethe, can't think of him as 'Tom'...
*The Magic Mountain*, in the unsure,
old translation, falls open at the same
page, night after night, in Intensive Care.

Propped up on mounds of pillows yet again,
I clutch the novel like a talisman,
a guide to health through labyrinths of pain,
or so I'd hoped, an ironic *Bildungsroman*

from which I could still learn, though sixty-four,
how thoughts might flower or intermesh at least.
TB for cancer, but one link seemed clear:
supposing you're well is when the blow is worst.

Hans Castorp's made it to the sanatorium
already, only as a visitor
for now, although there's so much more to come
– first hint is when he cannot savour his cigar.

And Settembrini, tracing luminous
ideals, prince of eloquence, is here...
and yet even he can't wholly mute the fuss
of tubes and drains and temperatures and fear.

And so I cling to this majestic work,
earning half-derisive wonder from my carers,
but notice, in the zero hours, that the book
has fallen like a burden from my fingers,

though something tells me, 'Stick with this; and find
a better version. It's more than just a novel.'
Electric lights keep me awake; consume each second.
Blankets rearranged, I'm Joachim's double,

honest and brave and stupid, and then I'm
Castorp's, naive, enquiring, and then I'm
Herr Director's, pragmatic, without shame,
and then I'm mine, tired, searching for a rhyme.

## SURGEON'S SON

Banged up in that place,
drains from three seeping wounds
turning crimson, red, yellow and God knows what colour
to the side of and under the bed,

enduring a chyle leak that had the team
scratching its high-powered, problem-solving head,
I boasted of you shamelessly,
my nonagenarian former surgeon of a father.

You'd been following the course of my op,
your shadowy presence a clasp of the hand
during the long, the semi-hallucinatory nights.
And it's because of you that I smiled,

a shade ironically, when the surgeons
were wondering whether 'to go back in'.
I said to a visitor, 'They're
like poets, itching to have another look,

to track down fault to a glitch
in the ligature, to a knotty
piece of not fully solvable,
oceanically complex bodily syntax.'...

After a drab Earls Court reading years back,
you came up to the bar, amazed
how easy it was, for once, to order a drink,
when the only competition was liquor-famished lyricists,

and commented quietly, 'I can see
your poems are the work
of a surgeon's son'...
'A surgeon's son who botches what he handles',

I half-joked, touched yet concerned
my own knife often cut my flesh and blood
too sharply. 'But thanks, anyway.'

You kept me going, banged up in that place.

## SHARK ATTACK

I'm tested, after a few days,
to ensure there's no gap,
no anastomotic leak
now my stomach's been hitched
to the stump of my oesophagus.

Hoisted on to a tilting
bed, swallowing evermore
indigestible gulps of barium,
I'm scanned from all angles; hang
in mid-air while something's checked.

The all clear's given; as a treat
at my request I get to see
ultrasound images of my gullet
and neck where lymph nodes
have been excised and harvested.

Almost a before and after diptych,
one side pulses away normally, but
the other side is criss-cross ravage,
cut into and about. 'Looked as if
I'd warded off a shark attack',

I say later, to laughter from the team
gathered round my bed, teasing me
about the crust round my mouth
– 'clear where you've been' – while I ham
up my sense of having been under assault.

Months on, I wake in the dead hours,
fingers at my throat, as though trying
to hold head, neck and torso in place,
and catch sight of a shark's fin, gliding
through a dark waste of waters.

## SHUNT

Took three sessions across three days of scalpel work
under local guided by computer imaging
to insert this thin tube that curves from my back
to my abdomen. Chyle circulating
through the tube, not swamping pleural spaces,
kept things in order and under control. It took
some doing. I saw the strain on faces
round me, heard the doctor say, 'Your skin's like teak,
plated, Clyde-built.' I did my best
but had to plead for greater pain relief,
feeling, all too keenly, the edge of the knife
as it cut my stomach first and then my chest.
The op did the trick. Surgeons removed the drains.
The leak had stopped. The tangible tube remains.

III

## ACHE

Waking at night, now at home, chest wound all of an ache,
I edge out of bed, my enteral giving tube trailing,
and make for my chair, then spoon down the pain-killing med.
My buttocky sore a spectacular annoyance,
bequest from the days and nights in bed,
I pick up my novel, read a few pages,
then turn to a volume I've not read for ages,
*The Earliest English Poems*, translated by Michael Alexander...
I identify keenly with exile and wracca (the wretched one)
beating lonely voyages over bitter-cold ocean,
the wanderer's lamenting *ubi sunt* questions:
'Where is that horse now? Where are those men?'
'Where is my stomach now?' I could well ask,
'now it's been pulled up, and I've been resected?
Am I the same, oesophagus rejigged,
tumour removed?' Complaint's half-indecent;
my only lost lord's my bodily wholeness.
I'm freed for a while – who knows how long? –
from cancer's consumption of organ and flesh.

## RECURRENCE

The latest word of fear
after such new familiars as 'scan',
'biopsy', 'bloods', 'nodes', 'leak', 'shunt'...

You lie awake most of the night, at home
after your release from Ward 36,
failing to act on your surgeon's advice:

'Try not to think about the risk'
– about as easy as not noticing
a skin-distending blood-clot on your left hand

or other randomly unmalign, you hope,
signs and portents. You lie here,
trying not to think about it,

mouthing the three syllables,
syllables as darkly intermeshed
as Atropos and co:

'recurrence' – the latest
word of fear, shadowy figure
glimpsed hurrying through cloisters,

possibly fleeing, possibly
approaching you, menace
visible in empty eye-sockets.

## ONLY NOW

'Similarly if you cut a man's head
down the centre', wrote Leonardo,
after describing an onion sliced
through the middle, so that all
the inner concentric circles show,

'you will cut through the hair first,
then the skin and the pericranium,
then the cranium' – and then, and then...
As my side-wound aches,
I imagine, two months after the operation,

the scalpel reaching the fascia,
pushing past deflated lung and separated ribs,
probing towards the malignant horror
at the core of my bodily self,
the anti-soul consuming me.

Only now, after weeks, does what I underwent
take on the form of a barely credible event;
only now have I to see myself, large fleshy
onion, dissected on a table; only now
can nightmare measure itself against grim fact.

## NIGHT FEED

I'd undo the purple-capped
toggle at the end of the JEJ line
that slid into my small intestine
before attaching the giving line
that offered me the latest enteral meal,
my sallow, yellow gruel,
to help me not lose too much weight
and keep nutritional goodness on the go.

I'd lie back on the heap of pillows,
listening to the silence and wheezing
the machine made as it pulsed slowly,
a regularly irregular sound
that seemed to be an inner ear disorder
when I first heard it in the ward.
Soon it'd be my bedmate night
after fitfully wakeful night.

Every couple of hours I'd trail
to the bathroom, carrying the machine
as though I were carrying a child
who will not yet must be lulled to sleep,
then wait for birdsong between five and six
while dawn would glimmer through the curtain
before the high-pitched peep of glad release
meant self-unmanacling could begin.

At first it was unbearable,
made me nauseous, fearful
of what might happen if the line slid out.
Finally I resigned myself, put up with treading
on the line – ouch! a sharp pang –
accepted it, a bosom

pal, however insensitive, however
glad the sight of its withdrawal made me –

the magical day when the specialist nurse
after getting me to lie down and lift my shirt
checked the stitches, realised they were torn already
and gently pulled the tube from my flesh,
its length increasingly green
as it slid out, no longer an intimate
companion – more like a snake's sloughed skin
briefly dangling, then consigned to a bin.

## LINES

*(i.m. Stephanie Dumke)*

Your husband – he who made
your face light up with happiness –
tells us, quoting *Adonais*
since you were so sensitive a scholar of Shelley,
that you slipped away a few days ago.

I met you first at the end of a public lecture.
You asked if I would be your supervisor.
There was something elfin, haunted in your eyes.
I felt I'd encountered a young woman out of Ibsen,
and said yes, and soon you came to work with me.

Restless, meticulous, a researcher,
you could not not be original:
Calderón and Goethe, their influence
the starting-point of your
fine, much-wrestled-with thesis.

You acted as my research assistant
(I felt I should have been yours), paused over
mistakes with forgiving disbelief:
'I think', you laughed, 'it's been
some time since you last read Aeschylus!'

You met the man you'd marry,
radiance enveloping your slender frame.
Papers and discoveries
flowered and you'd email me every now
and then to keep me posted.

Then silence, then confirmation cancer
had your life in its cell-dividing coils.
I'm glad we exchanged messages, just
months before your death, mine
eliciting what I want to write back to you,

'Can one really die, when
one receives emails like that?'
– write back and wait for your playful,
indomitable reply, telling me
with tactful pointedness I've made another

error, supposing you're not here.

## STUMBLE

A drizzling Easter Sunday. Resurrection
off the agenda, and yet you've risen
from your study's convalescent bed

to drag this new grief up the street.
You track with an invalid's slowness a route
you've known for years; each decade

blows away like a rain-surrounded vacuum
you watch head off behind you as your feet
move forward, testing out the lung

they had to deflate, ribs they had to spread and break.
You're still breathing, though, unlike that young woman
whose loss has shaken you, almost made you shake,

for whom the weather's turned elegiac,
while, out of puff, you imagine you're teaching yourself
futile persistence, how to stumble on.

## MAY

May, and this tree in blossom,
your five-year-old granddaughter
circling and circling the old trunk,

pink-white T-shirt a flicker
embracing the gnarled brown girth,
which served in stoic silence

as a goalpost decades back,
its partner long since chopped down
(the roots had threatened a drain);

branches soaring in crimson
abandon towards a sky
whose blue, receding, anchors

the infinite in the present;
and although you've just arrived
after weeks of illness, hours

of traffic jams, clogged-up miles,
it's as if you had been here
always, allowed to stare through

clusters of blossom at a
force you sense must lie beyond
whatever you imagine.

## CONVALESCENCE

… sitting on a maroon back
bench in the Half Moon
a little after five reward
for that overdue hour-long
pre-chemo post-op
visit to the dentist
hygienist giving my
gnashers the twice over

shadows pooled in
corners but the inner door
propped open to admit
wide slabs of light
salvifically silvering
cars, windows, passers-by

## DUMPING

Since much of my stomach
now serves as a substitute

oesophagus, pulled up
into my chest, it's not

been possible to eat
more than tiny portions,

before I'm reminded,
as in some grim fable,

of greed's dangers,
schooled if I overdo things

– an extra morsel, an unwise
forkful, a second bite –

by heavings
and nauseous pain

to regret any impulse
to exceed the rations

with which I must nourish
my rearranged self.

## BEAU'S LINES

Horizontal, ridged, indented furrows
score wavy tracks across my nails.
'Beau's Lines', the doctor calls them, showing
that when a breakdown's happened it prevails.

And yet, grooved relics of the pre-op chemo regime,
the lines will push towards the nail's top
higher and higher until it'll seem
disease has finally begun to stop.

Joseph Honoré Simon Beau
– name warranting stand-alone distinction –
explained their function long ago.

Cell-division slows, leaving datable
stigmata, before, if once more ill,
you'll search for signs of imminent extinction.

Intricate, immediate, intense,
its discipline enables violence
of feeling to permeate sonata form
and minuet. Triadic gusts, poised storm.
It has no time for sobs yet wrenches tears.
Key-changing shapes, musical mini-spheres,
arise and melt and reappear. If grief
is in the mix there's grace in each motif.

I played it every night whenever pain
woke me and had me retching yet again,
gasping for a morphine hit. As water turned
blood-red, I'd hear those violins accent
their sharp-sawed notes, that woodwind instrument
tell me all is counterpoint. Lesson learned…

Every night for more than a fortnight,
my left-on reading lamp torch-bright,

I'd dip into one of the Psalms,
recovery from sickness among their themes.

'All the night make I my bed to swim',
the author's faith placed touchingly in Him

– 'the Lord will receive my prayer'.
What held were swings between hope and despair,

the sheer intransigence of the text
('Let all my enemies be ashamed and vexed'),

words wrested from the spirit's distress:
'Shew thy marvellous lovingkindness.'

Switching the lamp off, I'd still see pages
scored through with cries of longing, its difficult stages,

its ultimate trust in its own truth:
'And he hath put a new song in my mouth.'

## SCAR

Sickle down my right side,
scored from well below my armpit
to the top of the back of my ribs.

To begin with, raw-red.
After weeks, a sabre cut
healing. To glimpse it disturbs,

queasily fortifies.
Thoracotomy's tattoo
traced twice over (after they

went 'back in'). The pain dies,
then throbs back, letting me know
the agon's on-going, won't go away.

Removing the final stitches,
the district nurse pointed out
their coarseness, fisherman's twine

almost – let's hope the catch was
all it might be, the net
crammed, leaving only this sign.

**FOCUS**

Fallen out of community
like a bundle of feathers from a tree,
you take to your bed once the next
'adjuvant' round of chemo begins to sing

melodies of malady. Things are happening
globally according to the slick
news channel. You're too sick
to respond more than numbly.

The poison pills – one large, one small – are pink.
Unwrapping them makes you retch.
Everything tastes like a platinum drink.
You can focus on that,

on your body's attempt to cope
with disrelishings, need for tonic water,
doseage control, and, sprung-syringe ritual,
jabs to boost neutrophil

numbers – 'remission'
possibly your best hope.

## NOTEBOOK

A listless pilgrim who mislaid
staff and scrip a long time back,
I drive, a fortnight
into chemo cycle 4, north
towards *insula sacra*.

Hold-up across the Tyne
but all's peaceable enough.
May blossom in Northumbrian
hedges and cloud-damped sunlight
look quotidian yet ethereal,

at least to the eyes of one
who's been through gruelling
surgeries and emerged to half-tell,
half-forget the grisly tale.
Stopping in castled Alnwick,

I think to check whether I left
a notebook bought in Majorca
a decade ago in my bag.
Imagine my consternation when,
unclasping the boot, I find,

instead of the bag, my excised
tumour, fibrous and bloody,
twitching like a landed fish
in its final convulsions,
a red-smearing tongue

owning the language,
lashing out, jeering: *You thought
you'd cut me out of your existence,
didn't you? My dimwit mate, you
thought you'd seen the last of me.*

I shut the boot in a fright, froze,
then opened it slowly, squinted
through the chink. Nothing there, only
old boots, a spare tyre, my bag with
this notebook, blank page uppermost.

## MIST-VEILS

Returning from the North Beach on Holy Island
where riders had guided horses along sand
until shapes veered off out of sight in an instant
as mist-veils dropped,

I can't shake off thought of how time seems
to have concertinaed since our first visit, of time's
slow work since we crossed the causeway's puddled gleams
and our spirits leapt

at such minstrelsy as I listen to now by the car,
bird song ascending and spilling, far
away as clouds one minute, the next as near
as rock that's been snipped

into jagged forms by wind and wet
– as near as a scar in the side of one's who's been got
at by healing knife, as a faith that belated regret
could never have started or stopped.

## TALL TALES

about Cuthbert's sanctity
come as relief of sorts
while I

deal with my own
uncanny miracle
– cut open and re-sewn

I think of the man of God
up to his neck in the dark
sea all night, spied

on by one of the brothers
who watches him kneeling
on the sand, dried by otters,

creatures blessed by him
before they immerse themselves
in their elemental home.

The brother confesses to Cuthbert
who forgives him, provided
he keeps his mouth shut,

which he did,
receiving a blessing in turn,
until the great man died,

when he started to blab
much as I've done since
release from suffering's lab

and the implicit invitation
to others to finger my wounds,
their verbal recreation.

## ANECDOTE FROM ITALO CALVINO'S 'WHY READ THE CLASSICS?'

Even as the hemlock was being brewed
Socrates was having a go at
a tune on the flute.

'What's the point of that?'
'At least,' he responds, 'before I die,
I'll have got the hang of this new melody.'

## TRIPLE TROUBLE

I'd come here twice or so a week,
fumble a sonnet on a masterpiece
but sometimes sensed a tremor after creak
of farewell shoe on floor. That unease

– it troubles me once more this afternoon.
Here's giant Ascanius shooting Sylvia's stag
against Lorrain's enchanted blue and green,
wrong foot (the right) extended, bow bent back.

I'm troubled much has altered, further
that little's changed. I've been ill, still can't draw
or body forth ideas in answerable tints.

That's two things troubling me – and, for the third,
there is this affectless state which has wiped out awe,
as though trash were the same as silk screen prints,

as though High Art lived somewhere I can't breathe
since the shapeless figure nicked me with his scythe.

## SHINING

My best time, these worse days
– 5 or so, the June morning
a huge bowl dripping with light,
a precious shining.

Birdsong more chorale
than throat-bursting racket –
it's possible to doze here in bed,
even read, to think one might again hack it,

to agree with my author,
'Nous avons fai du poison'
(he must have been thinking of chemo),
to imagine revival's horizon.

His tone, though – it's probably cutting.
Poison gives only a faithless guarantee.
What'd been silver has turned to cloud;
any song happens silently.

## YOU AND ONE

A friend reminds me Empson had it too,
cancer, that is, in his case of the throat,
although I read the lump
was possibly benign; by then he'd nailed

the recognition I've arrived at also:
'The method of cure is a scorched-earth
policy, liable to produce the
disease itself if you go on long enough'

(his 'you' still jaunty in the midst of dread);
'...lucky there is any method of cure of course'.
I'm pleased to find a main concern was not
being able to deliver some lectures which

colleagues, as they did for me, took on for him.
There it stops, random conjunction's casual web –
oh, and one last slight thread still quivers, 'how
very self-centred this disease does make one':

this time no 'you' in mind, save all of us.

## LAST SECTION

*'The camaraderie of carcinoma'*
ROY FULLER

Strange the stuff drifting in then out of thought:
*Available for Dreams* which I once thought
one of the finest ever vanished from
consciousness for years, until I bought it from
a seller for one p, plus postage – not
sure quite what motivated me though not
the sense I'd be rereading the last section
and inwardly exclaiming 'what a section!'
Entitled 'From the Cancer Hospital',
it takes you in and out of hospital,
the double sufferings of an elderly couple.
I read with too keen empathy; could couple
to that tale my chemo, surgery riot
through which his dry litotes might flare and riot.

## COMPLETING

Each line completing one thing and starting
another
      until the process breaks down
and the breath which seemed to rise
from the depths of the lungs just ebbs

away or stages a last-ditch
comeback and you're a garden windmill
gizmo whirling colours like a dancer

on a good day that is a day
when wind and sun are aligned
as they should be and health fights off illness and the
line you've just about completed catches

inflationary force and bellies outwards
and upwards towards a sky
                that makes
a mockery of our improvised shapings

that in turn soon surrender to
entropy and hearse themselves in the past

## WHAT'S THERE

Taking to my
bed after eating
a few mouthfuls

cramps in my stomach
curtains drawn barring
out the sunlight

through which people
drift in shorts and dresses
rejoicing in their

bodies' floral-patterned
health I think whimsical
*senex* of my long-lost

Brownie pinhole camera
through whose tiny
aperture one might

on a good day catch the
brave extravagant
bloom of what's there

**STOPPING**

Seem to have chosen to stop the chemo.
Toxicity too much, not enough will.
Can't keep going on even if it means I'll go.

The first day of July, ruthless light, no
cloud marring the blue. Dry-retching, weak, ill,
I seem to have chosen to stop the chemo.

Time in a daze as though on strike. So slow.
The oncologist tells me it can kill.
Can't keep going on even if it means I'll go.

I lie in bed, in a sunlit limbo;
a kind email regrets 'you've been through the mill;
perhaps you've chosen to stop the chemo?'

As though I believed some God-awful mumbo-jumbo
the sense of merited pain won't leave me still.
Can't keep going on even if it means I'll go.

My life before… no point in that, you know;
no need to be a retrospective fool.
Seem to have chosen to stop the chemo.
Can't keep going on even if it means I'll go.

**EXIT**

*(for Declan Kelleher)*


That old woman,
met when we sought the way at a door
between Sligo and Drumcliff
in order to cast a cold eye in the year
of arm-strapped Beckenbauer;

met like that figure in Joyce,
with her wispy white hair, bad teeth,
and wheezily resonant
'Sit you down boys and be at your ease;
I'll be back directly with your teas' –

that old woman decided
to tell our fortunes; I went second,
raw-boned cheeks in those days
as in these since I've been aligned
differently, foodpipe redesigned,

and heard, with a shiver of fear
that surprised me, the sentence
in both senses, 'you have the face
of one born to experience
great suffering.' Joking and tense,

I thought *suppose you have to shock
some of those whose features you scan.*
'That was strange, what she made of you'
my friend murmured as we began
our trek to Yeats's grave in the mild rain,

sunset a dull, dismal wound
slashed above the hills.
It all came back today at the airport
as, still not right, I swallowed a pill
and pondered throughlines to my recent illness.

*Please be aware that the nearest*
*exit may be behind you* we're
unreassuringly informed before take off.
She waits there, at all exits, a fortune teller
who knew the worst, stalking the future.

## PRAYER

By the waters that, navigated, link
Jersey to the Normandy coast
I half-collapse, nauseous
once more, on a ledge of rock,
new sun hat beating off glare,
and puke up a stream of bile
on to the firm, walkable sand.

My knuckles knot themselves
despite myself, an agnostic
disturbed to hear himself praying:
*Give me, O abdicated Lord*
*of hosts, give me the strength*
*to get through this (cue more retching),*
*to get through these difficult days.*

## CANDLES

1

Your emailed photos, each with a candle
newly lit among a ring of wicks
flaming less brightly, burning low,
managed those Sundays to kindle
a spherical teardrop of hope, letting me know
you'd thought of me, providing images
I could oppose to cancer's ravages,
visual cures, simples for the sick.

2

Verlaine received no solace from the view;
it made him ache with anguish and despair.
At the crammed marina in Saint Helier
I'm beginning to feel the same way too.

Sun could hardly be warmer, sky more blue,
but it's your candled stills that bring
worth at last to the day, deep colouring
not of this earth to my view of the view.

3

'Like darkness to a dying flame'
is the comparison, on the date its author died,
8 July, to which I'd allude
as showing the conflict image and rhyme

may lead to, in his case brilliantly. In the end,
though, is mine the condition of one who'd blunder
towards epiphanies of healing, blind
to the recurrent roguery of cancer?

I write this and yet what rises up, in my mind,
like a storm-battered lighthouse, a living beacon,
is the image of a candle shadows surround,
a self-nourished candle that tries to burn on.

## ANGUISH

*(after Verlaine)*

Nature, nothing about you stirs me, neither fields
that provide food, nor the rich-hued imitations
of Sicilian pastorals, nor dawn's recreations,
nor the doleful majesty of setting suns.

I mock art, human beings, and their songs,
verse, Grecian temples, and the corkscrew towers
cathedrals launch towards the emptied sky.
The good and bad are the same in my eye.

I don't believe in God, I abjure and renounce
all thought, and as for that old irony,
love, I wish no one would speak of it to me.

Weary of living, scared of dying, like
a lost toy boat at the mercy of ebb and flow,
my soul braces itself for an abject shipwreck.

## GONE

'Gone but not forgotten'
– so this bench proclaims
to the weary viator
strolling through thickening heat
round Saint Aubin's harbour.

'Gone and then forgotten'
– so my rewrite runs
as gannets plunge or float
and boats clink and rock
as though here for the duration.

Yet come high tide they'll inch,
expertly or awkwardly steered, inch
from their berths towards open
water, islands, clusters of rocks,
journeys that will soon

be forgotten, such as the one
I'm making now, still here
by the grace of the NHS, a
publicly funded survivor,
grateful for the respite,

however soon I'll be gone,
however quickly forgotten,
knowing the rare colour
this water yields – all rippling turquoise –
will greet the eyes of others,

also sitting with a drink,
staring towards a future
that will soon turn into a past
and yet remain a present, a shared,
atomised impression.

## MEANINGS

The way that, fleeting by, on a too full bus
you take in the blue of the famous bay
as though it were still the home of fabulous
myths where ocean deities might play,

– only myths seen too quickly, in a blur,
elusive as Eurydice's motives in looking back
over her shoulder at her dogged reclaimer
or the god's moment, as he saw it, of ill-luck

when Daphne's limbs turned into leathery bark –
the way that this is the case, if indeed it is,
tells you of meanings you'd be bound to miss

were you to head past an island towards the dark,
leaving Circe behind with her carmine nails,
sunset lingering like the snarl of her smiles.

# CODA

**PRESENCE**

Intermittent rain
drenches my jeans:
Tarn Hows again
ten months since

it had all seemed
close to over and out.
Then as now water gleamed
round each tree-clumped islet.

My moleskin hat, bought
to disguise shed locks, keeps
my post-chemo barnet,
its freshly curled loops,

dry as the bone
I began last year
to imagine
my whittled-down heir.

The blackthorn stick,
recruited when drop foot
briefly chose to inflict
itself, supports me right

to the car park
where we watch birds
furiously work
their bodies beyond words

into the flashing green
and blue of brilliant
colourings that define
presence, the moment.

## DOOR

I opened the bedroom door we rarely open
now my father sleeps downstairs. The shrine-like
cubic footage had the same parental odour.
The chair beside your dressing table,
with the mirrors in which I'd quiz
my adolescent profile, still sat there,
quite unaware of its contingent role
in your leaving – it was there, two years ago,
you found yourself bereft of breath,
your heart, that damaged, vivacious,
caring organ, having kept going
as long as it could.

I'd never noticed properly the books
you kept shelved at your beck and call
while preparing for the day's demands
or getting ready for the night
– books on depression and prayer, surely,
with the former, better to understand
others' suffering. Awful thing to say,
but thank goodness you died before my cancer
lifted the vile smirk of its cobra-head,
though, as always, you would have stuck
to your station, even if unable to sleep
for stabs of grief, and helped me tough it out.

I nicked – apols – your Bible Study 'Helps'
as a memento and, who knows, a guide
as well as this 'A7 Notebook'
which cost £1.75 and hadn't been used
until I pencilled in some lines, almost
with the hope you were watching me do so.
If you could, you'd have tracked the scrawl I traced,

been ready to intervene, as you did
when, perched on the long-vanished boiler,
you'd check my Latin verbs, and tell me
how to retread paths that had led to
waiting for 'viable' cells to multiply, to

staging a kind of séance with my mother.

## GHOST

That little girl
I was charged, with particular emphasis,
not to let run away,
kept, in my dream, with a laugh and a twirl
of long, black hair, doing just that,
even, once, blowing me a kiss.

I ended up, in one phase
of the night's oneiric adventure,
taking her to a film
we never saw, sent through the maze
blaring adverts constructed, which led her
to dart to the exit, almost disappear.

Then there was the time
she jumped from the back seat of the car
into a lane suddenly populated
by engines that dealt death – no rhyme
or reason for her act.
Crashing, I just about managed to save her.

I felt, with nagging acuteness,
post-op pain in my side when I had to chase
after her through an ever-widening,
ever-lengthening ballroom-cum-warehouse,
lagging behind as her legs stretched and quickened,
trying to catch sight of her phantom face.

Was it an allegory? I don't know.
Was she real? My soul? A loss of some sort?
What sticks in my head is the thump of my heart
the second I stopped running and the thought of snow
that falls and falls, of a mute, twirling fate,
of a mocking ghost that won't be taught.

## CHECK-UP

All going well, until the question:
'Have you drawn up a bucket list?'

*Item one*, I thought, *not to kick the bucket*,
but replied: 'No, I've not, not yet.'

Things I've not done and have no wish
to do; no exit with a flourish

via cruises in the Med; no ascents of
F6, 7, 8; no sudden remove

of my affections, work, routines;
no leaps from parachutes; no flying of planes.

'Just want', I add, a slight choke in my voice,
'to chug on as before',
                                    before this divorce

between me and my health, just want
to be well again, as I did when we sauntered

back to our holiday cottage in the Lakes
the summer I had my first taste of medics'

testing – in that case for a cancer
I turned out not to have, in prostate or bladder –

and heard a brook running off fells
while shadows like ghostly angels

peeled off the trees that swayed beside us
that evening we returned to an unlit house.

## THE STRANGER

*(after Baudelaire)*


'Whom do you love most –
Your father, mother, sister, or your brother?'

'I have no father, mother, sister, brother.'
'All right, which friend do you like best?'

'You use a word whose sense
remains a riddle to me to this day.'

'Does your country tug your heartstrings then?'
'Where such a place might be I couldn't say.'

'Do you love beauty best?' 'I'd love her
if she were divine and real.'

'Money?' 'Fills me with a fervour
of hate – the way you hate God.'

'So what *do* you love, you peculiar stranger?'
'I love clouds… the clouds that move… there

and there… each magnificent cloud.'

## LOVE

We sit, side by side, on a hotel sofa,
with pictures on the wall though this
time mainly still lives – fruit and listlessness.
Nothing to fret about or worry over

on this occasion, no dread
a surgical wizard will arrive late
in a green gown, tell me I'm not far off dead,
that last week's PET scan has unveiled my fate.

Those artless landscapes in the waiting room...
Now as you work your way through a catalogue,
scribbling left-handed notes, a couple's dog
stretched out on the rug, a bird's hymn

beyond the pane behind us, I resign
myself to the humdrum miracle of
being here still, writing another line,
sipping coffee, venturing the newly strange 'love'.

## AFTERMATH

*To unchain yourself from it all*
*to lift yourself out of date and place*
*but question that probably fake quasi-mystical*
*voice speaking as though it brought visions of grace*

*to chuck identity into the bin*
*to see with eyes no longer your own*
*to part from a self as boring as sin*
*to stare in a trance at a throne*

*crusted with stars in the evening sky*
*to watch from an upstairs window the white*
*wayward flight of a butterfly*
*above buddleia in fields of light*

*to surrender to sleep to surrender*
*let go give way yield quit the struggle*
*to shred the will in a powerful blender*
*to cease blowing full-cheeked through the ego's bugle*

*to unchain yourself from manacles of worry*
*to expunge from talk all mention of illness*
*to step aside from ambitions and hurry*
*to embrace pure nothingness stillness*

I write the above after treatment has finished
I write the above anaemic and tired
I write the above wanting 'I' diminished
taken to task admonished and fired

I glimpse a marvellous city
as though it embodied a single being magnified
and made from filaments of criss-cross electricity
that flowed then ebbed like a volatile tide

I have this glimpse then snuff it out as crazed
I think of perilous months when death seemed all too near
I dream of a mountain from whose summit a dazed
prospect rejects the slightest tinge of fear

I live again through fluorescent vigils
pain nausea attempts to be brave
I suffer once more three hospitals'
overwhelming commitment to save

me from replication of cellular
self-destruction I live through it all
my version of scorched-earth ruinous war
my broken resurrection unfortunate fall

I write the above a few months later
liver enlarged pain sharp unable to look at food
we all know what it means and the scan soon confirms cancer
my pal's again choosing this time a changed abode

prognosis initially weeks rather than months though
pain under control, I start to imagine I might...
why do I think these things be possibly among the one in two
who make it past the annual post and I start to repeat it

you know the stanza that goes
like a self-acknowledged ridiculous pose
like an attempt to hold wonder, ward off woes,
like a tune you feel could be sung by Mr Pobble's toes

*To stand in a field when mists begin to disperse*
*to breathe in air you'd not dared to hope*
*still existed to dispel the weight of the curse*
*to find you'd been somehow permitted to cope*

## TENSES

The tenses have ended
you head towards not
still a lot of you left yet

tiny jot of light
ready to be flayed and ended
shown how the track

might point out a track
a wide flame might
be minded to take

the tenses I think as
I swallow a pill
have not ended as

I turn on the heater
with its swoosh of air
the tenses have not

quite ended not
ended not
quite not quite

## HAMLET

'Goodnight, sweet prince.'
                    And yet it can't be good,
a night so kneaded and so thick with blood.
'Good night, sweet prince',
                    although you weren't so sweet
when one undid the other, love and hate.
But if the 'rest is silence', it's because
you fought, our hero, for a space, a pause
when the war between opposites might be
suspended in a form of purgatory.

Your bad dreams saved you, saved us with you too
– you looked from plot to life and dared to leap,
or dared us to think we might leap or sleep

or even dream, imagining 'adieu'
to all that's damped down on what's gone before
the fire, the ignorant, turbulent fire.

MICHAEL O'NEILL was born in Aldershot in 1953 and moved to Liverpool in 1960. He read English at Exeter College, Oxford and moved to Durham University in 1979 where he became Professor of English and Assistant Director of the Centre for Poetry and Poetics. He co-founded and co-edited *Poetry Durham* from 1982 to 1994. His most significant critical publications are on the topic of Romantic literature, and particularly the work of Percy Bysshe Shelley. One of his most recent critical books is, as co-author (with Madeleine Callaghan), *The Romantic Poetry Handbook*.

He received an Eric Gregory Award in 1983 for his poetry and a Cholmondeley Award for Poets in 1990. His four previous collections of poems are *The Stripped Bed* (Collins Harvill, 1990), *Wheel* (Arc, 2008), *Gangs of Shadow* (Arc, 2014) and *Return of the Gift* (Arc, 2018) and his poems have appeared in many journals and anthologies.

He died in December 2018, leaving a wife and two children.